ECOLOGY

Our Living Planet

Adapted from Steven Seidenberg's *Ecology and Conservation*

Gareth Stevens Children's Books
MILWAUKEE

P. HOGAN

For a free color catalog describing Gareth Stevens' list of high-quality children's books call 1-800-341-3569

Library of Congress Cataloging-in-Publication Data

Hogan, Paula Z.
　　　Ecology: our living planet / Paula Hogan and Steven Seidenberg.
　　　　　p. cm. — (My first reference library)
　　　Bibliography: p.
　　　Includes index.
　　　Summary: Presents for the primary level a survey of pressing issues of conservation as they affect our entire planet and everything living on it.
　　　ISBN 0-8368-0030-3
　　　1. Ecology—Juvenile literature. 2. Nature conservation—Juvenile literature. 3. Pollution—Environmental aspects—Juvenile literature. 4. Biosphere—Juvenile literature. [1. Ecology. 2. Conservation of natural resources. 3. Pollution.] I. Seidenberg, Steven. II. Title. III. Series.
　　　QH541.14.H63　　　1989
　　　333.7'2—dc20　　　　　　　　　　　　　　　　　　　　　　　89-11282

North American edition first published in 1990 by
Gareth Stevens Children's Books
RiverCenter Building, Suite 201
1555 North RiverCenter Drive
Milwaukee, Wisconsin 53212, USA

Photographic credits: Aspect Picture Library 23; Susan Griggs 51; John Hillelson 14 (bottom), 21 (bottom), 28; Jimmy Holmes 49; Magnum 5, 11 (top), 25, 38; Massey Ferguson 17 (top); D. C. Money 32, 50; Marion and Tony Morrison 9 (top), 14 (top), 16 (bottom), 45; Natural Science Photos 11 (middle and bottom), 12 (bottom), 37, 39, 48, 58, 59; Oxford Scientific Films 12 (top), 35, 36, 43, 53; Panos Pictures 27, 42; Planet Earth 57; Robert Harding Picture Library 21 (top); Frank Spooner 17 (bottom), 30, 31; Telegraph Colour Library 4; Thames Water Authority 33.

Illustrated by David Holmes and Eugene Fleury

Series editor (UK): Neil Champion
Series editor (US): Mark Sachner
Editor (US): Rita Reitci
Research editor (US): Scott Enk
Educational consultant: Dr. Alistair Ross
Editorial consultant: Neil Morris
Design: Groom and Pickerill
Cover design: Kate Kriege
Picture research and art editing: Ann Usborne

Printed in the United States of America

1 2 3 4 5 6 7 8 9 96 95 94 93 92 91 90

Contents

1: ONLY ONE EARTH

The Living Planet

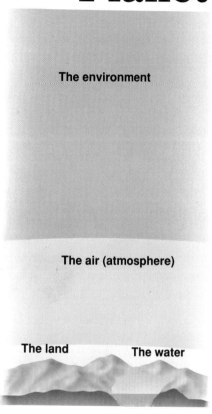

The environment

The air (atmosphere)

The land The water

▲The environment of Earth has three zones of life: the air, or atmosphere, the land, and the water. Earth is the only known planet that supports life.

This picture shows the blue oceans, the brown land, and the white clouds of Earth. ▶

Earth is the only known planet that supports life. Plants and animals can live here because the environment has air to breathe, water to drink, and weather that is neither too hot nor too cold. Plants and animals live in three zones, or places, on Earth: the air, or atmosphere, the land, and the water. These zones interact so that life can go on.

The Water Cycle

Every living thing needs water. The water cycle shows how the air, land, and water interact.

Water vapor cools down and forms clouds   Rain falls on the land

Rivers take the water back to the sea

Water evaporates and rises

Oceans and seas
328,891,337 cubic miles
(1,370,000,000 cubic km)

Ice
5,761,600 cubic miles
(24,000,000 cubic km)

Lakes and rivers
55,215 cubic miles
(230,000 cubic km)

Atmospheric vapor
3,361 cubic miles
(14,000 cubic km)

◀ The water cycle. The Sun heats water. Some water evaporates. It rises into the air and cools to form clouds. Water in clouds falls back to Earth as rain. Rain runs into rivers. Rivers flow to the sea.

The Sun heats up the water in lakes and oceans. Some of the heated water evaporates and rises into the air. High up, the water cools to form clouds. The water later falls back to Earth as rain. The rain runs into rivers, lakes, and oceans.

People Are Threats

People change Earth by cutting down forests, polluting the air and water, and letting deserts get bigger. Earth could change so life is not possible.

▲People are polluting Earth more and more. This picture shows a beach ruined by oil spilled from a huge ship. Birds and fish living near the spill may die.

The Web of Life

In an ocean food chain, krill eat tiny plankton. Small fish eat krill, then become food for larger fish. Seals eat large fish, and people eat seals. ▼

Food Chain (I)

There are millions of different kinds of plants and animals on Earth. Each kind, or species, has something special that makes it different from all others.

Elements of Life

All plants and animals need four elements to live. Plants take these elements in through their roots. They also use sunlight to change elements into food. Animals eat plants or plant-eating animals to get these important elements.

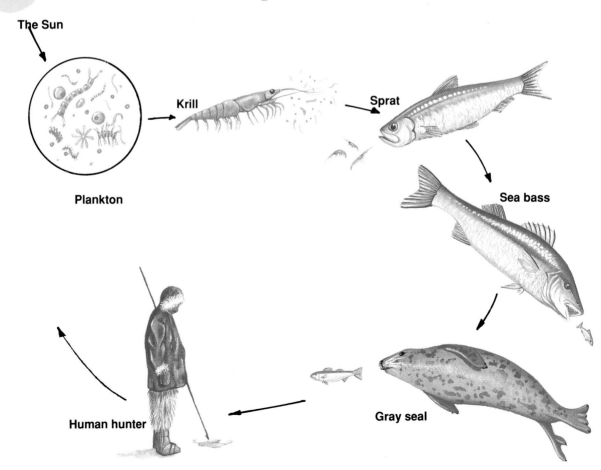

The Sun

Krill

Sprat

Plankton

Sea bass

Human hunter

Gray seal

The Food Chain

Animals cannot live without plants. They are linked together by a web of life called a food chain. Each living thing is food for another living thing.

Food chains are easily broken. For example, if farmers use pesticides to kill harmful insects, the shrews that eat the insects don't have enough to eat. Many shrews will die, and the owls that eat shrews will go hungry. The owls might die out, too.

In a forest food chain, caterpillars eat tree leaves. Small birds eat caterpillars, and birds of prey, like the hawk, eat the small birds. When the hawk dies, insects like the beetle feed on its body. The insects help break down the hawk's remains so that they enrich the soil. Trees grow better in rich soil.▼

Food Chain (II)

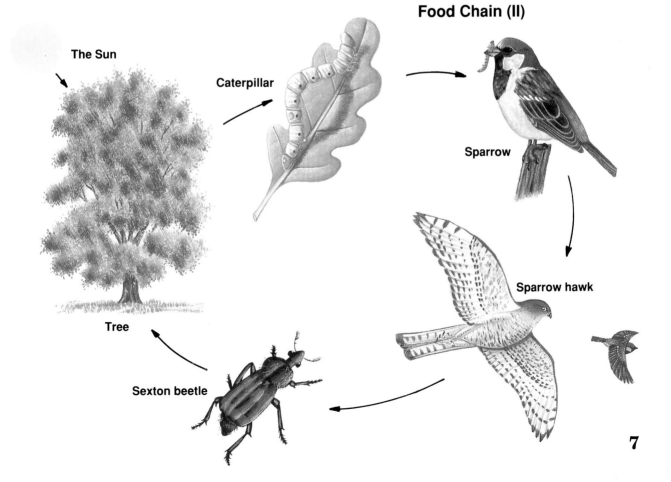

The Sun

Caterpillar

Sparrow

Sparrow hawk

Tree

Sexton beetle

Pollution

Acid rain hurts forests. Look at the insert. How is the healthy pine tree branch different from the branch hurt by acid rain? ▼

Pollution hurts the environment. Humans pollute the air with smoke and gases from cars and factories. They dump garbage and harmful chemicals into rivers, lakes, and seas. They pollute the soil with fertilizers and pesticides.

Acid Rain

Factories and cars give off poisonous smoke. When these poisons mix with water in the air, they form a weak acid. Then

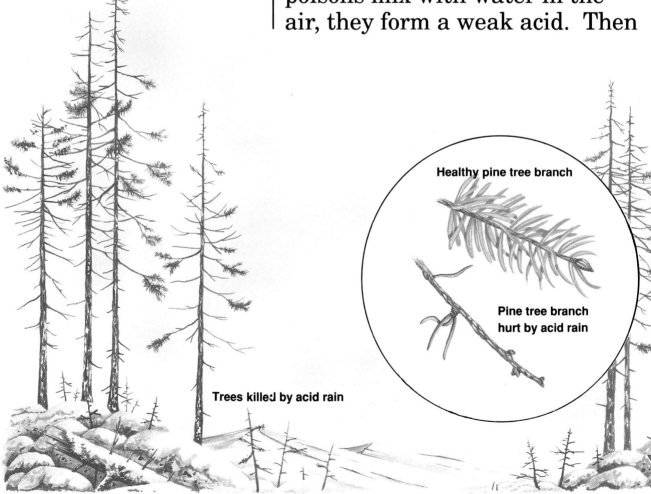

Healthy pine tree branch

Pine tree branch hurt by acid rain

Trees killed by acid rain

the water falls to Earth as acid rain. Acid rain damages buildings. It kills plants and fish. Acid rain clouds can travel for hundreds of miles. So acid rain can cause damage far away from the factory smoke that started it.

Stopping Pollution

Pollution is hard to stop. People want cars. They want things that are made in factories. People must learn to do without some things, and scientists must find ways to stop factories from polluting the air.

▲A smoky fog, called smog, hangs over Mexico City. Smog is not healthy to breathe.

Oil and chemicals in the water and garbage on the shore have ruined this beach environment.▼

2: PLANET EARTH

The Earth's Crust

Rivers carry tiny pieces of rock, called sediment, to the sea. ▶

Soil is the top layer of our planet, and it is part of the Earth's crust. Most of the world's plants and animals live in or on the soil.

Soil is a mixture of broken rock and dead plants and animals. These materials trap water and air. They also provide food for tiny life forms called microbes that live in the soil. Dead plants and animals, together with microbes, make soil fertile so that other plants can grow.

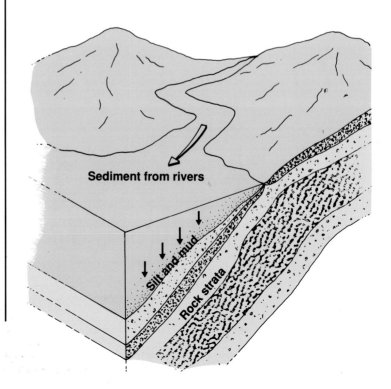

Sediment from rivers

Silt and mud

Rock strata

Making Soil

It takes many years for soil to form. Wind and water break rocks into tiny pieces so that they become part of the soil. This is called weathering, and it acts very slowly. It takes 100 years to make half an inch (1 cm) of soil. Erosion takes away soil much faster than weathering can make it. People who use land carelessly cause most erosion. They allow wind and water to carry soil away. People cannot make new soil. Only weathering can. People must use land in ways that keeps erosion from happening.

▲There are many kinds of environment on Earth's crust. Cold Antarctica, fertile farmland, and rain forests are some examples of the variety.

Inner core
Outer core
Mantle
Crust

◀ Earth's inner core is surrounded by three outer layers.

Soil Life

The midwestern US (right) has rich soil. The African Sahel (opposite) has poor soil. ▶

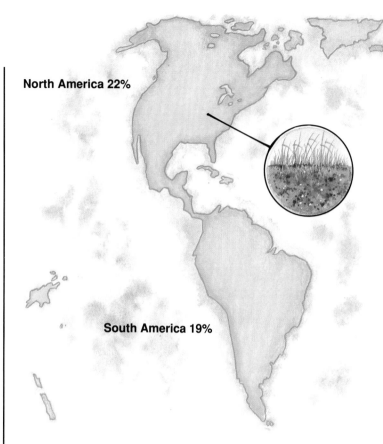

North America 22%

South America 19%

▲Earthworms (above) and wood ants (below) make soil rich. They break down dead plants and animals into bits of soil.

Good soil is full of life. It is home to tiny animals like worms and insects. Soil also contains microbes, living things too small to see without a microscope. Just a spoonful of soil may hold hundreds of millions of microbes. That soil also includes over 4.6 billion fungus cells.

Tiny animals and microbes enrich the soil. Worms, for example, help break bits of rock into even smaller pieces. Worm tunnels allow air and water to get into the soil.

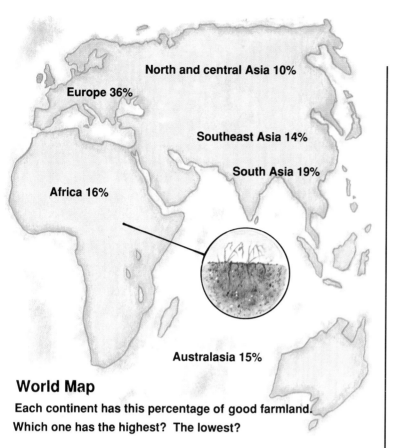

World Map
Each continent has this percentage of good farmland.
Which one has the highest? The lowest?

North and central Asia 10%

Europe 36%

Southeast Asia 14%

South Asia 19%

Africa 16%

Australasia 15%

Some microbes help trap gases that plants need to grow. The food chain starts with microbes. No plants or animals can live without microbes.

Different Soils

Most soil is not good for farming. It may be too cold or too wet. Sometimes soil is not deep enough. Many soils don't contain enough microbes or tiny animals. Some countries have more good farmland than others. But erosion strips away good land everywhere.

Facts & Feats

Some life forms need to be in surroundings that would kill other life forms, including humans. There are bacteria that live where there is no air!

The rich soils in northern China and the Mississippi Valley can be 500 feet (152 m) thick. Norway has very thin soil. It averages 4 inches (10 cm) thick.

There are 3.7 billion acres (1.5 billion hectares) of farmland in the world. Every year erosion ruins 2.5 million acres (1 million hectares).

Rich soil produces four times as much food as poor soil.

Farmers in the United Kingdom and Japan use 45 times as much fertilizer per acre as Nigerian farmers. So one acre (0.4 ha) of land in these countries grows six times as much grain as an acre in Nigeria.

Only about two-thirds of the world's farmland is used to grow food. The rest is used for grazing animals.

Losing Ground

▲Farmers cleared these hillsides of plants and trees so they could grow food. The rain washed the soil from the bare slopes.

We cannot live without healthy soil. Yet, people destroy about 10,000 acres (4,000 hectares) of soil every day. When soil is destroyed, we cannot make more.

Erosion
One way soil is destroyed is by erosion. Wind and water carry soil into the ocean where it disappears forever.

Plants help protect soil. Their roots and leaves keep wind or rain from washing soil away. Often, farmers clear protective plants from the soil.

Dust storms happened in the western United States during the 1930s. Bad farming methods left the soil uncovered. Strong winds blew it away in huge black clouds. ▶

Water erosion

Wind erosion

Overgrazing and Irrigation

Animals such as sheep, goats, and cows eat grass. When too many animals graze too long in one spot, they make the ground bare. Then the soil erodes away.

Farmers use irrigation to bring water to dry fields. Good irrigation drains away unneeded water. Too much water kills plants and harms soil. Some irrigation water is salty. The salt stays in the soil and kills crops.

▲Wind erodes the soil by blowing it all away. Wind can shape bare rock in strange ways (right). Water can wash away soil and carve deep gullies (left).

Did You Know?

After farmers harvest their crops, they leave the soil bare. Wind and water can then easily carry soil away. Crops growing in rows leave the most soil bare.

Saving the Soil

These terraces in Peru slow down the rainwater. When water flows more slowly, it carries away less soil. ▼

The fastest way to stop erosion is getting farmers to follow good farming practices.

Stopping Erosion

Strong winds blow the soil away. When farmers plant windbreaks of trees and hedges, they slow down the wind. They slow down erosion, too.

Rainwater builds up speed as it runs downhill. The faster the water flows, the more soil it carries away. Rainwater can be slowed down by building terraces. Contour plowing across

Did You Know?

For a long time farmers have known about building terraces to stop erosion. No-till plowing is a new idea that some farmers are using to stop erosion on their land.

◀ This farmer is practicing no-till plowing. Instead of cutting deep furrows, the plow drills seeds into the ground.

These windbreaks keep soil from blowing away. Between the breaks, small plants grow. Their roots help hold the soil down so that more plants may grow. ▼

the path of running water also slows the water down so that much less soil will wash away.

New Plowing Methods

When a farmer plows his fields, he buries the crop stalks and leaves the land bare until it is time to plant once more. Now some farmers are trying no-till plowing as a way to stop erosion. They plant their seeds in very shallow furrows or drill them into the ground. The cut stalks from last year's crop stay on the field. The ground is never left uncovered, so wind and rain can't carry much soil away.

3: THE BREATHING PLANET

The Air

Earth is wrapped in a huge layer of gases. We call this layer the atmosphere. The gases in the atmosphere make up the air that we breathe.

The atmosphere helps us in other ways. In the daytime, it blocks out harmful radiation from the Sun. At night it acts like a blanket, keeping the Earth warm. The atmosphere also protects Earth from meteorites. Most meteorites

Plants breathe in carbon dioxide and breathe out oxygen. Cows breathe in oxygen and make wastes after eating plants. Their wastes contain nitrogen, which helps new plants grow. ▶

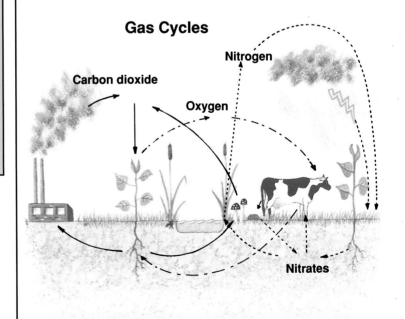

Gas Cycles

Nitrogen

Carbon dioxide

Oxygen

Nitrates

18

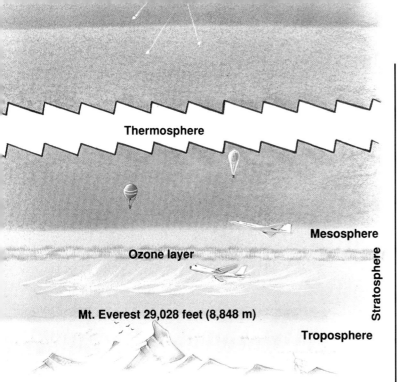

Thermosphere

Mesosphere

Ozone layer

Mt. Everest 29,028 feet (8,848 m)

Stratosphere

Troposphere

◀ The atmosphere is divided into layers. The layer closest to the Earth is called the troposphere. Most of the atmosphere's gases are in the troposphere. Other layers are the stratosphere, the mesosphere, the thermosphere, and the exosphere.

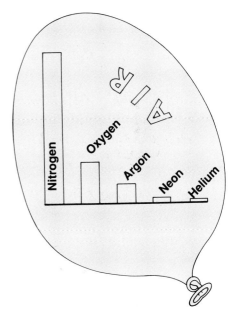

AIR

Nitrogen

Oxygen

Argon

Neon

Helium

▲The atmosphere is made up of many gases.

burn up in the atmosphere before they hit the ground.

Gases in the Atmosphere

There are many different gases in the atmosphere. Only three gases exist in large amounts. Nitrogen, oxygen, and argon make up 99.9% of the gases in the atmosphere. Smoke, dust, water vapor, and even microbes also float in the atmosphere. The atmosphere gases are thickest at sea level. At 300 miles (480 km) up, they are almost gone. Most of our weather takes place in the thick layer of gases closest to the Earth's surface. This layer is called the troposphere.

Did You Know?

The environment is divided into three parts: the air (atmosphere), the land, and the water. The atmosphere is larger than any other part of the environment. Gases from Earth are found over 600 miles (965 km) above sea level.

The Human Cost

Pollution occurs when wastes called pollutants get into the air. Most wastes come from things people do. Pollutants can harm humans, plants, and animals.

Pollutants

Pollution comes from burning fossil fuels such as coal, oil, and gas. Burning fossil fuels releases harmful gases into the air. Tiny bits of liquid, soot, and dust also discharge into the air when fossil fuels are burned. Harmful gases also come from factories and from burning solid wastes.

Facts & Feats

In 1952, over 4,000 people in London died of air pollution. Now new laws keep London air clean.

Each year factories in Europe give off 40 million tons of sulfur dioxide, a polluting gas.

Acid rain has killed almost half the fish that lived in the lakes of southern Norway.

Over half the trees in West Germany's Black Forest are damaged by acid rain.

The Acid Rain Cycle

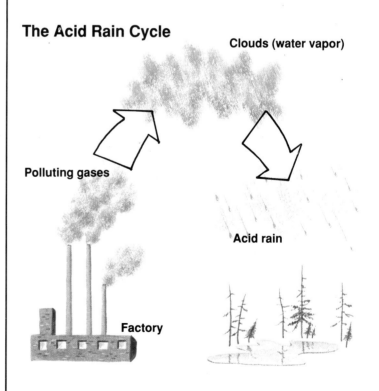

Clouds (water vapor)

Polluting gases

Acid rain

Factory

The acid rain cycle. Gases get into the air and mix with water vapor to form acid clouds. The clouds release acid rain. ▶

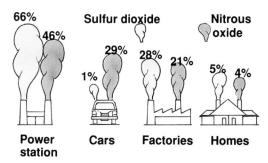

66%	Sulfur dioxide		Nitrous oxide
46%	29%	28% 21%	5% 4%
1%			
Power station	Cars	Factories	Homes

◀ Air pollution in Athens, Greece, is among the worst in the world. Greek temples that are thousands of years old are falling down because air pollution is eating away the stone.

In Japan, the air pollution is so bad that many people wear masks to help keep it out of their lungs. ▼

Fossil Fuels

We need to burn fossil fuels to run our cars and power our factories. Fossil fuels also provide energy to heat our homes and to make electricity.

Acid rain occurs when pollutants from fossil fuels mix with water in the air. Together they form clouds of acid. These clouds may drift for hundreds of miles before they fall to Earth as rain. Acid rain kills plants. It runs into rivers and lakes, where it kills fish and other water animals. When it falls on cities, it eats away at stone buildings.

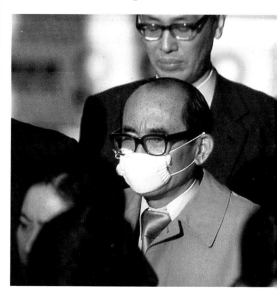

Polluted Poland

Poland is one of the most polluted countries in the world. Polish coal is of poor quality, so it releases lots of harmful gases.

Polluting the Air

The greenhouse effect. Burning fossil fuels releases too much carbon dioxide into the air. Just like the glass in a greenhouse, carbon dioxide lets the Sun's heat in but it doesn't let it out. This causes the weather to get warmer. ▼

Air pollutants form other deadly products besides acid rain.

The Greenhouse Effect

When we burn fossil fuels, we release carbon dioxide into the air. Plants need to breathe in carbon dioxide. But too much carbon dioxide in the atmosphere will turn the Earth into one big greenhouse. Greenhouses let in the Sun's heat but keep it from going out. If the Earth becomes like a greenhouse, the air will get hotter and hold more water, so less rain will fall. Many food crops may no longer grow.

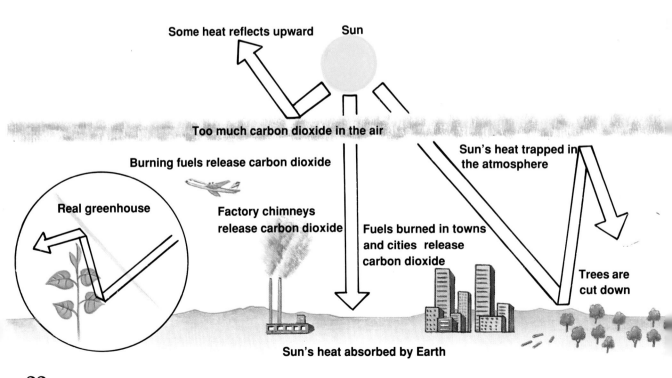

Some heat reflects upward   Sun

Too much carbon dioxide in the air

Burning fuels release carbon dioxide

Sun's heat trapped in the atmosphere

Real greenhouse

Factory chimneys release carbon dioxide

Fuels burned in towns and cities release carbon dioxide

Trees are cut down

Sun's heat absorbed by Earth

◀ Smoky fog, called smog, is made up of several pollutants. One of them is ozone. Los Angeles is the smoggiest city in North America. In this picture, the smog is so thick that it makes the sky look brown.

◀ Chemicals (CFCs) from refrigerators, some spray cans, and fast food cartons can destroy the ozone layer.

Ozone

Ozone is a special form of oxygen. At ground level, it harms crops and forms smog. An ozone layer lies 15 miles (25 km) above Earth. This layer stops much of the Sun's harmful radiation. Without the ozone layer, this radiation would reach Earth and harm plants, animals, and humans.

Ozone

Chemicals made by people can mix with the ozone layer and destroy it. These chemicals, called CFCs, keep our refrigerators cool. They are sometimes put in spray cans as a gas. They also make up the foam plastic packages used for hamburgers and other foods.

Cleaning the Air

There are several ways to stop air pollution. Power stations should use only high quality coal and oil. These fuels cost more, but they burn cleaner. Power station chimneys need scrubbers to trap pollutants before they reach the air.

Engines and Chemicals

Newer engines cut down the amount of pollutants released into the air. Engines using lead-free gasoline lower the amount of lead put into the air. Cars, trucks, and buses can have devices that trap pollutants to keep them out of the air.

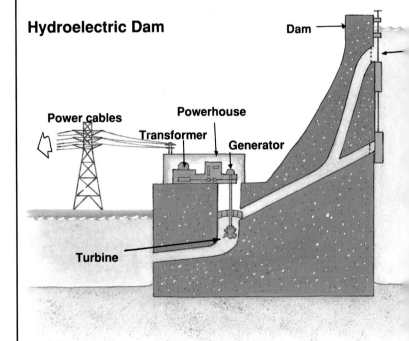

Hydroelectric Dam

Dam

Power cables

Powerhouse

Transformer

Generator

Turbine

Water power is a clean way to make energy. When water from behind the dam flows out, it turns a turbine. The turbine makes electricity. ▶

Some countries now limit CFCs, the chemicals that destroy the ozone layer. The US bans using CFCs in spray cans. Canada and some other nations limit the amount of CFCs they make. This helps, but we need to do more. We need to find other chemicals to take the place of CFCs.

The Cure

We can all help stop pollution. We can stop buying spray cans using CFCs and goods wrapped in foam packages. We can use less electricity. We can walk more, instead of riding in cars.

▲Wind power is another clean source of energy. These wind vanes in California use the power of the wind to make electricity.

Did You Know?

People are working on clean sources of energy. Wind power provides electricity in California. Wave power and tide power make electricity in other parts of the world. Solar energy uses the Sun's warmth to heat many homes.

4: A WATERY WORLD

A Blue Planet

Water covers two-thirds of the Earth's surface. ▶

Facts & Feats

The Nile, flowing 4,160 miles (6,693 km), is the longest river in the world.

The Amazon River has the world's largest river basin. It covers an area of about 2.7 million square miles (7 million sq km).

Every second, 6.3 million cubic feet (178,000 cu m) of water flows from the Amazon River into the sea.

Lake Superior in North America is the world's largest freshwater lake.

The deepest freshwater lake is Lake Baikal in the USSR. It goes as far as 5,315 feet (1,620 m) down.

About 76,650 cubic miles (319,000 cu km) of sea-water evaporate and fall as rain each year.

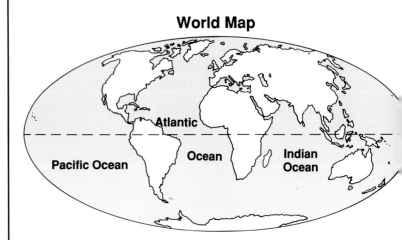

World Map

Atlantic

Pacific Ocean

Ocean

Indian Ocean

When seen from outer space, Earth looks like a blue planet. This is because over two-thirds of Earth's surface is water. Plants and animals can't live without water. Water exists only in environments with the right temperature range. If it's too hot, water changes into steam. If it's too cold, water freezes.

The Water Cycle

Water keeps moving through the air, the land, and the seas. We call this the water cycle. Heat causes water in rivers, lakes, and oceans to change into vapor.

Plants give off water vapor. The water vapor rises into the air, where it forms clouds. When the water vapor in clouds cools, it goes back to liquid form. Then the liquid falls to Earth as rain or snow. In time, this water runs into the oceans. Then the water cycle begins again.

More than 97% of Earth's water is in the seas. Seawater is salty. Most land animals and plants need fresh water to live. Of all water, less than 3% is fresh water.

We use water in many ways. We need it to move goods and people by boat. We use it to irrigate croplands. We have fun in water when we swim, surf, or sail. In this picture, women from Sri Lanka are getting salt from seawater. ▼

Life in the Sea

▲This special submarine helps scientists find out more about life deep under the sea.

The oceans of the world all flow into one another. Together they form one big ocean. The surface of the world's waters is twice as large as that of the land.

The Oceans

The oceans are the largest and deepest zone of life on Earth. Some land animals can live several feet below ground, but sea life can exist over 2.3 miles (3.7 km) below the surface of the ocean! Animals and plants live in all parts of the ocean. Some, like jellyfish, live on the surface.

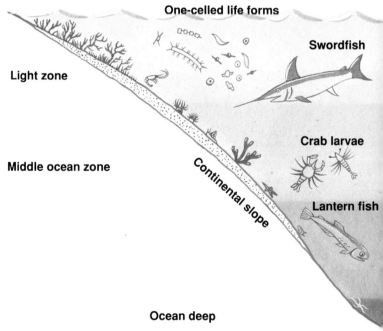

One-celled life forms

Swordfish

Light zone

Crab larvae

Continental slope

Middle ocean zone

Lantern fish

Ocean deep

Others, like most fish, live in the middle. At the bottom you can find sponges, clams, and other plants and animals. Nine out of ten species, or types, of life that live in the oceans live on the ocean floor.

Life in the Oceans

Even though the oceans form the largest zone of life, not many different types of things live in them. The ocean has only about 20% of Earth's life forms living in it. The rest of the Earth's species live on land or in the air.

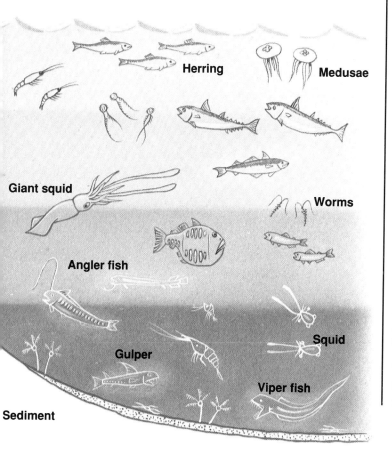

Herring

Medusae

Giant squid

Worms

Angler fish

Squid

Gulper

Viper fish

Sediment

◀ Ocean layers. The ocean can be divided into different layers by what lives there. In the top layer, sunlight still penetrates the water. The ocean deep is entirely dark, and luminous fish and other animals there have to make their own light.

Water Pollution

We need water to drink and to grow food. We eat fish and other animals that live in water. We get salt from the sea. We take oil and natural gas from under the sea floor.

Wastes in the Water

Even though we need water, we pollute it in many ways. We dump human wastes in rivers. We dump garbage into lakes and oceans. Many factories dump chemicals and other dangerous materials into rivers and seas. It is cheaper for factories to just dump wastes without making them safe first.

Farmers use chemical fertilizers and pesticides to help their crops

Every day this barge takes garbage from New York out to sea. When the barge is far from shore, it dumps the garbage in the ocean. ▼

grow. Rainwater washes these chemicals into rivers and lakes. This makes the water unsafe for humans and kills animals and plants living in those waters.

Oil Slicks

Oil pollutes the water if it is spilled by accident or dumped as waste. When lots of oil enters the water, it floats on the surface to form a slick. Slicks may cover huge areas. Oil slicks kill many animals living in or near the sea. A spill from a single large tanker may kill up to 30,000 sea birds, as well as countless other sea life.

▲This river looks clean, but it is very polluted. A papermill pours waste chemicals through a pipe into the water.

▲These animals died because their water home was polluted.

Keeping the Waters Clean

▲ In China, people grow mulberry bushes to breed silkworms. The bushes need clean water supplied by irrigation.

This plant removes toxic waste from sewage. After treatment, the sewage can safely be flushed into rivers and seas. ▶

There are many ways to keep rivers, lakes, and oceans clean. Sewage and human wastes can be treated before flushing them into the environment.

Dangerous Chemicals

Some chemicals can be treated like sewage before they are pumped into the sea. Other chemicals must be burned at high temperatures. Dangerous materials, like radioactive wastes and harmful chemicals, are put in special containers before they are dumped in the ocean. Some of these containers have started to leak. It would be better not to put them in the sea.

The Mediterranean Sea

Not long ago, the Mediterranean Sea was very badly polluted.

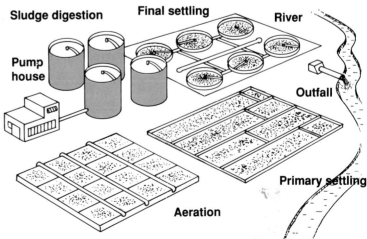

Sludge digestion   Final settling   River

Pump house

Outfall

Primary settling

Aeration

The pollutants were trapped because the sea is almost completely landlocked. This made beaches unsafe. It was dangerous to eat seafoods like mussels and clams. It seemed that all the sea life would die.

In 1976, almost all the countries surrounding the Mediterranean agreed to stop dumping wastes. Today there is less pollution, but we still have a long way to go.

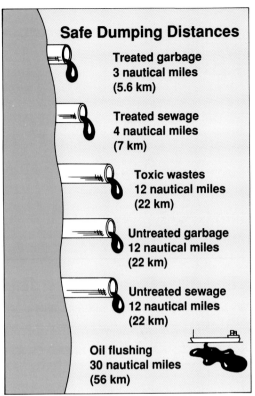

Safe Dumping Distances

Treated garbage
3 nautical miles
(5.6 km)

Treated sewage
4 nautical miles
(7 km)

Toxic wastes
12 nautical miles
(22 km)

Untreated garbage
12 nautical miles
(22 km)

Untreated sewage
12 nautical miles
(22 km)

Oil flushing
30 nautical miles
(56 km)

▲This chart shows how far from shore boats must go before they dump wastes off the coast of Britain. Other countries may permit dumping either closer or farther from their shores. A nautical mile is longer than an ordinary mile. It equals 1.15 miles (1.85 km).

◀ This river was once polluted. Now that it's clean, fish can live in it again. Cleaning up polluted waters is very costly.

The Deserts

Facts & Feats

About 200 million people live in the dry lands surrounding deserts.

The Sahara Desert, the world's largest desert, covers an area almost as big as the United States!

Sahara sand dunes can be 1,410 feet (430 m) high.

Some deserts have sand, some are almost all gravel. Others have a rocky floor, and some are made of ice.

Nearly half the world's deserts are in cold regions. Antarctica is the largest cold desert.

Libya recorded the highest temperature ever in 1922. The thermometer read 136.4°F (58°C).

A true desert gets less than 10 inches (25 cm) of rain each year. Few people live in deserts because they are so dry. Deserts and the dry lands that surround them make up one-third of the Earth's land surface.

Desert Temperatures

Lack of rainfall makes desert air very dry. There is no moisture, or humidity, in the air to block out some of the Sun's warmth.

World Map

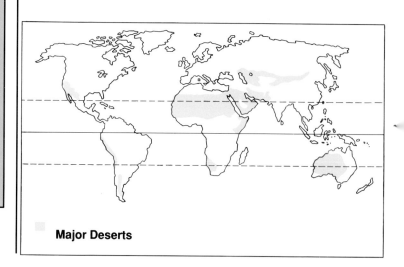

Major Deserts

The rain shadow. Mountains keep moist air from reaching the land beyond them. Little rain falls on that other side.

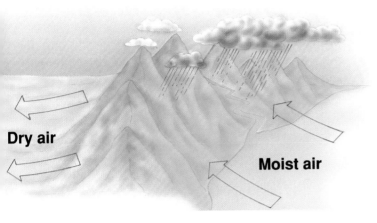

Dry air

Moist air

▲This picture shows the Kalahari Desert blooming after a rain storm. Desert plants grow fast after a scarce rainfall.

With so much heat reaching the ground, deserts become very hot by day. But at night, desert temperatures fall very low. This is because there is no humidity in the air to keep the heat from escaping. Places with more humid climates have a smaller change in temperature from day to night.

Plant Life

Desert plants have short growing seasons. In hot deserts, plants grow only when there is rain. Cold deserts warm up above freezing for only a few weeks each year. Cold desert plants can grow only during this short time.

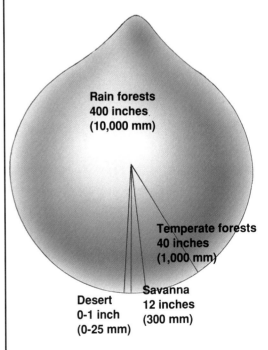

Rain forests
400 inches
(10,000 mm)

Temperate forests
40 inches
(1,000 mm)

Savanna
12 inches
(300 mm)

Desert
0-1 inch
(0-25 mm)

▲Rain forests get the most rainfall each year and deserts get the least.

Types of Deserts

We usually think of deserts as having sand dunes like these, but most deserts do not. Only a small number of deserts are covered with sand. ▼

Tropical deserts are hot all year round. Subtropical deserts have hot summers and cooler winters. Some subtropical deserts have freezing temperatures in winter.

Cold Deserts

Cold deserts are covered with ice even though very little rain or snow falls during the year. The little snow they get almost never melts. It stays on the ground year after year. In polar deserts, all the water is frozen, so almost no plants grow there. Tundra deserts do have a short summer. Then the temperature rises high

enough to melt some of the ice.
Then a few hardy plants get
enough water to grow.

Why Are There Deserts?
Most of the moisture in the air
comes from evaporating sea-
water. Some lands are dry
because they are far from the
sea. Sometimes the moisture
falls as rain before it can reach
these lands. Other deserts exist
because dry winds blow across
them all year round. Rain
shadows are another way to
form deserts. Mountain ranges
block the flow of moist air. The
moist air falls as rain on the sea
side of the mountain. The air
that blows down the other side
of the mountain is dry.

▲Stony deserts like this
one are common around
the world.

The temperature is below
freezing year round in
polar deserts. Even
though very little snow
falls, it never melts.
Year after year, the snow
builds up. ▼

Marginal Lands

Partly dry, or semiarid, lands get more rainfall than deserts. But there still isn't enough rain to grow forests or crops. Usually semiarid regions are covered with grass. They are often called marginal lands.

Grasslands

There are two main types of grasslands: savanna and steppe. Savannas are grassy plains in tropical and subtropical regions. Steppes are also grassy plains, but they are in colder regions. Steppes have hot summers and cold winters. Savannas are warm the year round. Some savannas have wet and dry seasons.

The Mongols and the Kazakhs are two groups of people living on the steppes of Siberia. They roam with their herds that feed on the grass of the steppes. ▼

Food Crops

Semiarid lands are marginal in two ways. First, they exist on the margins, or edges, of deserts. Second, they are marginal because only a small amount of food can be grown on semiarid land. Crops must be watered through irrigation.

Farmers can't use the same fields every year because the soil needs time to enrich itself. If the same land is used several years in a row, the soil will become more like desert land.

▲During the wet season, this savanna in Kenya becomes very green. Many wild animals drink at this water hole when night falls.

Upsetting the Balance

The Dust Bowl

In the early 1900s, US farmers plowed up the marginal grasslands of the Great Plains. They planted crops like wheat and corn. Then dry years came in the early 1930s. Winds blew away tons of soil in huge clouds. The clouds blackened the sky as far as the Atlantic Ocean. An enormous area, called the Dust Bowl, became ruined for farming and grazing. This was one of the biggest environmental disasters in the world.

Grassland provides good pasture for livestock. Nomads live here, people who move from place to place to find food and water for their herds. As long as their animals don't stay in one place too long, the grassland is not harmed. Erosion occurs if the animals eat all the grass. Then the bare soil is carried away by wind and rain.

Too Many People

With more people in the world, farmers need to grow more food. Often they must use marginal land for crops, so there is less land for pasture. More animals feeding in a smaller area will eat all the grass and turn the pasture into desert.

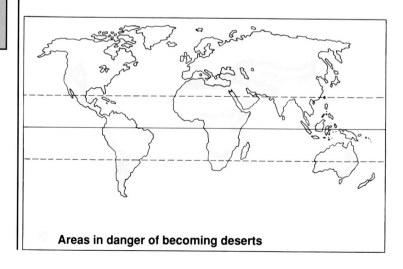

Areas in danger of becoming deserts

This map shows the main areas of the world in danger of becoming deserts. ▶

40

Worn-out Soil

Grassland soils are too thin for farming. Crops can only grow for a few years before the soil wears out. Then good grass cannot grow there to feed livestock.

▲Nomads live in deserts and marginal lands by raising cattle, sheep, and other grazing animals. Today it is hard for them to find enough food and water for their livestock. ▼

Stopping Desert Growth

Changes in natural climate can make deserts grow bigger. There is nothing we can do about that. But humans also turn good land into desert, and we can keep this from happening. We can't grow enough food for everyone if there isn't enough land to grow it on. Over half of the land that erosion turns into desert every year is grassland. This pasture for livestock is lost.

Facts & Feats

Over 23,000 square miles (60,000 sq km) of soil becomes desert each year. This is nearly the area of West Virginia.

Each year 80,500 square miles (208,500 sq km) of land loses its ability to grow crops. This area is about the size of Kansas.

Over one-third of the Earth's surface is desert or affected by desert growth. Six percent of the Earth's land is close to becoming desert.

Africa has many deserts. Bad farming practices have forced many people to use land that is not good for crops.

These desert people are ▶ digging a well to get water.

The Green "Great Wall"

Older Forest

Advancing Gobi Desert

Recently planted forest

CHINA

The Green "Great Wall"

Long ago, forests were cleared in northern China to make way for farming. Now erosion is destroying the land. The Chinese are fighting erosion by planting a green "Great Wall" of trees. They plan to plant bands of trees across the whole country.

Deserts Get Bigger

Deserts can spread quickly. Bad farming methods and over-grazing will cause a small patch of desert to appear. The good land that is left is plowed by more farmers and grazed by more animals. Soon more and more patches of desert appear. In time, the patches link up, turning a whole region into a desert. Land on the edges of deserts has the greatest risk of turning into desert.

Dangerous Goats!

The best way to stop desert growth is to keep farmers from changing pasture into cropland. Herds of animals that graze on marginal land must not be too large. Only the right kind of animal should be allowed on grasslands. Goats, for example, are commonly kept grazing animals. They are very hardy but they do great harm to marginal land. They eat everything and leave the ground bare.

◀ After eating all the plants on the ground, this goat climbed a tree to get more.

43

6: THE GREEN BLANKET

The World's Forests

This map shows where the largest rain forests are found. ▶

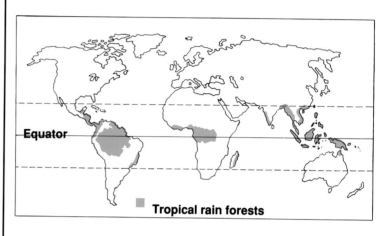

Equator

■ Tropical rain forests

Forests Make Oxygen

We need forests to make oxygen, an important part of the air we breathe. Plants breathe in carbon dioxide and give off oxygen that goes into the air.

Trees Protect the Soil

Tree roots help bind grains of soil together. This traps rain water, slowing it down. Slowing down rain water stops erosion. In rain forests, the canopy of leaves acts like an umbrella. The leaves protect the forest floor from the hot tropical sunlight and the strong rains.

44

Recycling Water

Forests help recycle water. In a process called transpiration, trees and other plants take up water from the ground. This water brings nutrients from the soil to the plants. The trees and other plants later release the water through their leaves into the air. The water sent into the atmosphere forms clouds. Later, the water falls as rain and soaks into the soil. This happens over and over again.

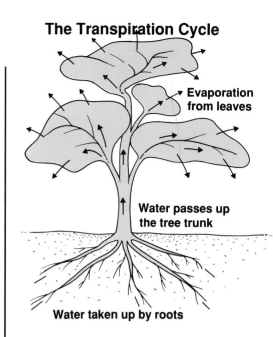

The Transpiration Cycle

Evaporation from leaves

Water passes up the tree trunk

Water taken up by roots

▲ Trees take up water through their roots. The arrows show where the water goes out from the tree leaves and into the air.

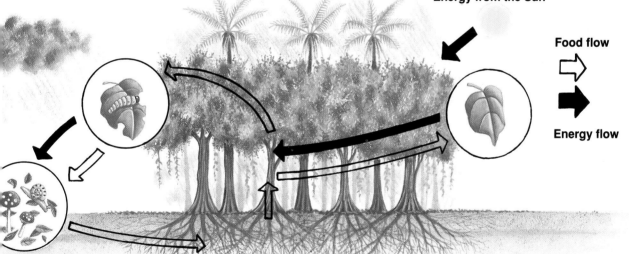

Energy from the Sun

Food flow ⇨

Energy flow ⮕

▲ Rain forest tree leaves make food from sunlight. Dead leaves and animals enrich soils to help trees grow.

◀ Clouds over the hill forests of Peru are part of the water cycle.

45

Different Forests

Facts & Feats

Tropical rain forests cover 16% of the land surface, but they contain half the species of all living things.

Over half the world's total rain forest area lies in three countries — Zaire, Brazil, and Indonesia.

It rains heavily in rain forests. A rain forest in Ghana may get more rain in 15 minutes than San Francisco gets in an average month.

More kinds of trees grow around one volcano in the Philippine rain forest than there are of native trees in North America.

Bamboos, woody grasses common in rain forests, can grow up to 24 inches (61 cm) in a day!

Tropical Rain Forests

Jungles are called tropical rain forests. They grow where the weather is hot all year long and a lot of rain falls. About half of all forests are tropical rain forests. Several thousand kinds of trees may grow in rain forests. The trees have broad leaves that stay green all year.

Temperate Forests

Temperate forests grow in areas with cooler temperatures and less rainfall. In winter the trees lose their leaves. Huge temperate forests once covered Europe and the eastern part of the United States.

Coniferous Forests

Coniferous trees bear cones, and they have small, needle-shaped

Squirrel monkey

Jaguar

Different Kinds of Trees

Coniferous trees

Temperate forest trees

Rain forest trees

leaves that stay green all during the year. The trees grow where the winters are long and cold and the summers are short. Even very large coniferous forests have only a few different types of trees.

▲Coniferous trees have needle-like leaves. Temperate and rain forest trees have broad leaves.

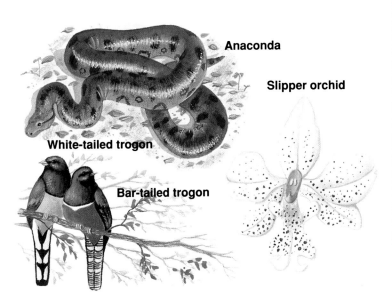

Anaconda

White-tailed trogon

Bar-tailed trogon

Slipper orchid

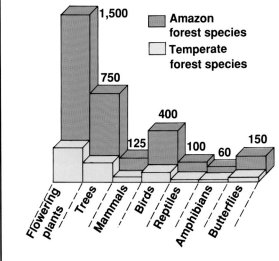

◀ These are some plants and animals of the rain forest.

47

Cutting Down Trees

All over the world, forests have disappeared. Thick forests once covered Europe and the Middle East. Little by little, people cut down trees until now almost no forests are left. North America once grew some of the largest forests the world has ever seen. By 1860, nearly 90% of the forests in the United States were gone because people had cut down the trees.

During the last 90 years, people have cut down almost half the world's rain forests. Today we lose about 150 acres (60.7 ha) of rain forest every minute. This

▲Bulldozers cut roads into the thickest rain forests. Farmers move in along these roads and clear fields to grow animals and crops.

Each year there are more people, so more food must be grown. Farmers, like this one in Morocco, cut deeper into the forests to make more fields. ▶

means that every second a forest about the size of two football fields disappears!

Farmers clear away forests to make room to grow crops or graze animals. Other people cut down forests to get the wood. People also build cities and roads on land that was once forest.

Erosion

Without tree roots to hold it together, the soil washes or blows away. When people cut down trees, other forest plants and animals also die.

▲People use wood to build houses, furniture, and boats. Many people must burn wood for cooking and heating.

▲Baskets of firewood for sale in Nepal. People in Nepal use wood for fuel. That is why their forests are disappearing.

Saving the Trees

▲ This pawpaw plant grows in South American rain forests. The green fruit turns orange when it ripens. Like other useful plants, it will disappear if the rain forest is destroyed.

The rain forest floor. Rain forest soil is very thin. Most nutrients come from the leaf and plant litter on the top. ▶

People cut down forests to get fuel, timber, and farmland. The temperate forests in Europe and North America were the first to be destroyed. Now we protect forests in these areas and plant new ones.

Today, rain forests are in danger. Once a rain forest is cut down, it is gone forever. Unlike temperate forests, a rain forest cannot be replanted.

Even though many plants grow in a rain forest, the soil is quite poor. Most of the nutrients the plants need come from dead plants and leaves rotting on the

Leaf litter

Clay soil

Rock

50

This rain forest in Brazil was cut down for timber. People are planting tiny seedlings. They hope to start a new forest and protect the soil from erosion.

forest floor. The warm, humid weather in the tropics speeds their decay. Cutting down trees takes away nutrients on the forest floor. All that's left is a thin layer of soil too poor to grow plants. Without plants to cover the soil, wind and water carry it away. The rain forest soon turns into a desert.

Hugging Trees

In northern India some people are trying to save their forests. Members of the Chipko movement hug trees to keep loggers from cutting them down with axes and saws.

New forests now cover this once open land. ▼

7: WILDLIFE
New Species

Guenon monkeys

▲These rare guenon monkeys live in Madagascar.

The rosy periwinkle from the Amazon rain forest may give us a new medicine. ▼

Nobody knows just how many different kinds of living things there are on Earth. Scientists have named 1.5 million species so far. Millions more are still to be discovered. Most unknown species are plants and insects that live deep in rain forests.

Useful Wildlife
Different kinds of plants and animals can be very useful to

humans. About 25% of all our medicines come from plants. The rosy periwinkle, for example, grows in the Amazon jungle. It contains a cure for some kinds of cancer. Another Amazon jungle plant produces a fluid called methanol. We can use methanol in place of gasoline. We are using up so much oil to make gasoline that we may need this plant.

There are many other plants in the Amazon jungle that we don't know about. Maybe some of these unknown plants can help people. But many of these living things may die out before we get a chance to learn about them and how we can use them.

The jojoba plant lives in North American deserts. The berries produce a very fine oil that can be used in place of whale oil. This plant could help keep whales from being killed. ▼

53

Wildlife in Danger

Many kinds of plants and animals have disappeared. They have all died and become extinct. Most often extinction happens because of human actions — hunting or changing environments.

People Cause Extinction

Extinction is happening today at a faster rate than ever before.

Animals made extinct since 1650

	1650	1700	1750	1800	1850	1900	1950	2000
Mammals	4	2	3	5	3	30	46	
Birds	2	3	4	8	14	45	45	

▲ This time line shows the number of birds and mammals that became extinct over seven periods of 50 years each.

In the past, humans caused the extinction of only about one species a year. Since 1985, humans have been at fault for the extinction of about one species each day!

Long ago, most of the animals killed off by humans lived on islands. When humans arrived at these islands, they brought livestock along. Sheep, pigs, and

Did You Know?

Plant species are in danger, too! About 10% of all US plant species are in danger of extinction. In Hawaii, nearly 250 plant species have disappeared and nearly 1,300 more are in danger of dying out.

cattle took the places of the native animals and made them extinct. Rats on sailing ships swam ashore and killed off whole species of ground-living birds and other kinds of animals. Today, it's not just island wildlife that is in danger. Extinction threatens plants and animals all over the world.

The passenger pigeon, last seen in 1914

The dodo, last seen in 1700

▲ The dodo and the passenger pigeon are just two species of birds humans have hunted to extinction.

◀ Endangered species. Plants and animals of all kinds are under threat of extinction. ▼

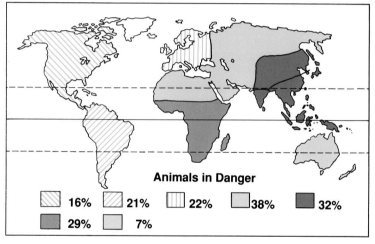

Animals in Danger

16%　21%　22%　38%　32%

29%　7%

Humpback whale

Large blue butterfly

Panda

White rhinoceros

California condor

Snake's head fritillary

55

Extinction

▲ The North American bison, or buffalo, once covered the Great Plains in huge herds. People hunted them close to extinction during the 19th century.

Bamboo and the Panda

If a single plant species dies out, as many as 40 other kinds of insects, animals, and other plants can be in danger. The giant panda eats only one kind of bamboo. With more land being cleared for crops, there is less land for the bamboo to grow on. If this kind of bamboo dies out, so could the giant panda.

Hunting

People hunt animals for food and for sport. Some types of whales have been hunted so much that very few are left. The North American bison once lived in huge herds. Hunters killed thousands for sport, and the bison almost disappeared.

Some animals are hunted for their valuable skins. Leopards, tigers, and other big cats die so their fur can be made into coats. People hunt certain crocodiles, alligators, and snakes because their skins make beautiful shoes, wallets, and handbags.

New animals that come into an area endanger the native species. Cats brought to islands to kill rats also ate the native birds. Sheep, pigs, cattle, and goats that come in use the land, the food, and the water, so there is not enough for the native animals.

Destroying Habitats

A habitat is the environment where a species lives. Habitat change is the biggest cause of extinction. Cutting down rain forests and clearing grassland for farming destroys wildlife. Many species can only live in one type of habitat. When their habitat changes, they die.

▲ Demand for goods made from fur and reptile skin could cause the extinction of some animals.

Facts & Feats

Some scientists believe that dinosaurs died out because a prehistoric rat ate the dinosaurs' eggs.

Some experts say that Stone Age people hunted the mastodon and the woolly mammoth out of existence.

Nearly 1,000 kinds of animals and over 20,000 species of plants are endangered.

In Java, only about 50 Javanese rhinoceroses are still living.

◀ Many kinds of whales have neared extinction from overhunting. Only the Japanese and Soviets still hunt whales.

WILDLIFE

Saving the Future

Old Faithful Geyser in Yellowstone National Park shoots boiling water into the air. Yellowstone was the world's first national park. Now there are over 2,000 more in countries around the world. ▶

National Parks
There are over 2,000 national parks and wildlife reserves in the world. In Africa, Kenya and Tanzania earn money from their national parks. Many tourists visit them to watch and photograph the wildlife.

Protecting Wildlife
Most plants and animals die out because people destroy their habitat. We must preserve their habitat by protecting forests and keeping marginal land from turning into desert. Humans must make good use of the farmland they have before they try to farm land that is not as good for growing crops. Wildlife

58

preserves and national parks protect wildlife habitat. These areas cannot be cleared for farming. Hunting is against the law, and very few buildings or roads can be built.

Zoos and centers for endangered species preserve some species under threat by helping them breed. Zoos are breeding a kind of antelope that was hunted almost to extinction in Arabia. Some of these antelope born in zoos now live free in Arabia.

Many countries have laws that protect wildlife. These laws make it a crime to hunt or sell endangered species.

▲The European bison once neared extinction. A few lived on in zoos. Now young bison raised in zoos range freely in a Polish national park.

Wildlife reserves, like this one in Africa, are the last hope for species that are close to extinction from overhunting. ▼

Glossary

Acid rain: Rain that contains acid. It forms when pollutants, such as sulfur and nitrogen oxides, combine with water vapor in the atmosphere.

Acids: The common acids are sour-tasting chemicals that can burn flesh. Many acids can kill plant and animal life and can eat into substances like glass, metal, and concrete.

Atmosphere: The layer of gases around an astronomical body. The atmosphere of Earth is made up mainly of the gases nitrogen and oxygen, as well as tiny amounts of carbon dioxide and other gases.

Carbon dioxide: A gas made up of carbon and oxygen. Humans and animals breathe carbon dioxide out, and green plants take it in to use with sunlight for making their food. Burning fossil fuels produces carbon dioxide.

CFCs (chlorofluorocarbons): Chemicals made of carbon, hydrogen, chlorine, and fluorine. Until lately, CFCs were widely used in refrigeration and spray cans. Because they endanger our atmosphere, many countries now ban or limit their use.

Contour plowing: Tilling the soil so that the plow follows the natural curve of the land, making furrows across slopes. Plowing in this way reduces erosion of the soil.

Elements: The different basic substances from which all known matter is made. Each element is made of only one kind of atom. The elements most important to life are nitrogen, oxygen, carbon, and hydrogen.

Environment: Our surroundings; the things that affect the way a person, animal, plant, or other living thing lives.

Erosion: The slow wearing away of the Earth's surface by things like wind, rain, glaciers, wave action, and flowing water.

Evaporate: To change from liquid into a gas or vapor.

Exosphere: The outermost layer of Earth's atmosphere. Atoms of atmospheric gas easily escape from this layer into space.

Extinct: No longer existing. Species of animals that do not exist any more, such as dinosaurs or the dodo, are said to be extinct.

Fertile: Producing good crops. Fertile soil is rich in the materials plants need for healthy growth.

Forestation: Planting trees to establish a forest; also, the care of forests.

Fossil fuels: Fuels made naturally from the remains of plants and animals that lived millions of years ago. Coal, oil, and natural gas are all fossil fuels.

Great Wall, the: A massive wall in China, built centuries ago to protect the land from invasion. Today, the Chinese people are creating another great wall, a green "Great Wall" to protect their land from erosion.

Greenhouse effect: The warming of Earth's atmosphere or climate because of increased carbon dioxide in the atmosphere. The atmosphere then acts like a greenhouse, trapping the Sun's heat. This can change our weather, especially by making it drier, because hot air holds more water without rain falling. The excess carbon dioxide comes mainly from burning fossil fuels.

Habitat: The area or surroundings where a living thing or group of living things is usually found.

Hectare: A unit of area in the metric system equal to 10,000 square meters, or nearly 2 1/2 acres.

Irrigation: Watering land or crops by using streams, canals, or pipes. With irrigation, farmers can grow crops in places that do not have enough rainfall or other natural sources of water.

Krill: The name given to many different kinds of small shrimplike animals that live in all oceans.

Marginal: At the edge, being on the margin or at the limit. Marginal lands are commonly found in the partly dry, or semiarid, regions of the world, often on the edges of deserts.

Mesosphere: The layer of Earth's atmosphere found between the stratosphere and thermosphere. The mesosphere lies 30-50 miles (50-80 km) above Earth's surface. Its temperature falls rapidly as you go higher in it.

Meteorites: Lumps of metal or stone from space — remains of meteors that have fallen through Earth's atmosphere to its surface.

Microbes: Living things so small they can be seen only with the aid of a microscope. Bacteria and viruses are two common types of microbes.

Nitrogen oxides: Gases made up of nitrogen and oxygen, often released when fossil fuels burn. One form, nitrogen dioxide, comes from automobile exhausts and can mix with water vapor in the atmosphere to form acid rain.

No-till farming: a method of farming by leaving crop remains on the soil and planting seed in drills or very shallow furrows. Keeping the ground covered at all times protects it from erosion by water and wind.

Nutrients: Substances that provide nourishment. Food is the main source of nutrients for people. Plants get most of theirs from the soil.

Ozone: A form of oxygen made up of three atoms in each molecule instead of the usual two. A layer of ozone gas lying about 12-15 miles (19-24 km) above Earth's surface protects all living things from the harmful ultraviolet radiation from the Sun. CFCs damage this protective layer. This lets more ultraviolet radiation reach Earth, where it can cause skin cancer in humans and can also harm plants and animals.

Pesticides: Poisonous substances that kill animal or insect pests. The buildup of pesticides in the environment is an ecological problem.

Plankton: Very tiny living aquatic plants and animals. Some live in the ocean and some live in fresh water. Most are microscopic.

Pollutants: Undesirable or harmful substances that poison the environment. Pesticides, factory wastes, sewage, smoke, and nuclear radiation are some of the most common pollutants.

Radioactive: Discharging rays or particles of atomic energy. There is no way to destroy radioactivity. Radioactive wastes must be sealed in special containers.

Savanna: A grassy plain in hot regions of the world with few or no trees. There are savanna lands in Africa and South America.

Scrubbers: Devices that trap harmful pollutants and make them harmless. Some scrubbers in chimneys keep harmful gases from getting into the atmosphere.

Semiarid: Partly dry. Most semiarid land gets enough rain to grow grass, but not enough for growing farm crops.

Species: A group of animals, plants, or other organisms that are alike enough physically to have offspring just like them.

Steppe: A dry, grassy plain without any trees and located in cool regions of Earth.

Stratosphere: The layer of Earth's atmosphere between the troposphere and the mesosphere. It lies 10-30 miles (16-50 km) above Earth's surface. The ozone layer lies within the stratosphere. The temperature of the stratosphere rises as you go up.

Subtropical: Lying near the borders of tropical zones.

Sulfur dioxide: A bad-smelling gas, often released by burning fossil fuels. It can combine with water vapor in the air to form acid rain.

Thermosphere: The layer of Earth's atmosphere between the mesosphere and exosphere. It lies 50-400 miles (80-640 km) above Earth's surface, and as you go up, its temperature may rise up to 390°F (200°C).

Toxic: Poisonous. Many of our wastes are toxic and they can poison the air, the water, and the soil, unless they are somehow made harmless.

Transpiration: The evaporation of water from plants.

Tropics: Hot areas of Earth, generally lying between two imaginary lines, also called tropics, drawn around Earth. One tropic line lies north of the equator, and the other lies south of the equator.

Troposphere: The lowest layer of Earth's atmosphere. It goes up to about 10 miles (16 km) over the tropics and 5 miles (8 km) over the Earth's poles. The air temperature falls as you go up until it reaches from -110°F to -60°F (-79°C to -51°C). Nearly all of Earth's weather takes place in the troposphere.

Tundra: The huge, flat, treeless plains of the Arctic lands, a few areas of the Antarctic, and in mountain regions. Tundra is different from steppe because its ground beneath the topsoil is frozen all year round.

Waterlogged: Soaked with water. When the soil becomes waterlogged, the plants growing in it usually die. Rice grows in wet soil, but most food crops will not grow in waterlogged soil.

Weathering: Wearing away through the action of wind, water, sunlight, heat, cold, and plant and animal life.

Windbreak: A row of trees, shrubs, or fencing that protects something from the full force of the wind. Windbreaks are useful ways of fighting wind erosion.

Index

A **boldface** number shows that the entry is illustrated on that page. The same page often has text about the entry, too.